D1468829

The UNIVERSE'S GREATEST DINOSAUR JOKES

and PRE-HYSTERIC PUNS

Artie Bennett

STERLING CHILDREN'S BOOKS
New York

To the wonderful Jennifer Berne,
no dinosaur she

STERLING CHILDREN'S BOOKS
New York

An Imprint of Sterling Publishing Co., Inc.
1166 Avenue of the Americas
New York, NY 10036

ISBN 978-1-4549-2984-0

Distributed in Canada by Sterling Publishing Co., Inc.
c/o Canadian Manda Group, 664 Annette Street
Toronto, Ontario, M6S 2C8, Canada
Distributed in the United Kingdom by GMC Distribution Services
Castle Place, 166 High Street, Lewes, East Sussex, BN7 1XU, England
Distributed in Australia by NewSouth Books
45 Beach Street, Coogee, NSW 2034, Australia

For information about custom editions, special sales, and premium and
corporate purchases, please contact Sterling Special Sales at 800-805-5489
or specialsales@sterlingpublishing.com.

Manufactured in Canada

Lot #:
2 4 6 8 10 9 7 5 3 1
01/18

sterlingpublishing.com

Cover and interior design by Ryan Thomann
Cover images from iStock: © 21kompot (wave); © Grytz (dino);
© Hotspur (reptile pattern)

Contents

Who filled prescriptions during prehistoric times?

Tyrannosaurus Rx.

Which dinosaur was always on time?

Pronto-saurus.

Which dinosaurs were known to spin around and around for relaxation?

Tricera-tops.

Why did Utahraptor always chomp on automobiles during his rampages?

Because he was a *car*-nivore.

Why were Stegosauruses popular at dinner parties?

They brought their own plates.

Why should you *never* take a dinosaur bone on the New York City subway?

You'll jostle your fossil.

Which dinosaur chose word power over brute force?

The Thesaurus.

Which dinosaur appeared in prehistoric rodeos?

Bronco-saurus.

And what do their riders get if they compete too long?

Saddle 'saur.

Where do dinosaurs still follow cavemen?

In the dictionary.

Which dinosaur . . .

. . . wore a sombrero?

Tyrannosaurus Mex.

. . . wore a ten-gallon hat?

Tyrannosaurus Tex.

. . . pumped iron?

Tyrannosaurus Pecs.

. . . played cards?

Tyrannosaurus Decks.

. . . could put a curse on you?

Tyrannosaurus Hex.

. . . wore eyeglasses?

Tyrannosaurus Specs.

. . . did yoga?

Tyrannosaurus Flex.

. . . just broke up with her boyfriend?

Tyrannosaurus Ex.

. . . believed that England should withdraw
from the European Union?

Tyrannosaurus Brex.

. . . was *sooooo* irritating?

Tyrannosaurus Vex.

. . . always picked up the tab at restaurants?

Tyrannosaurus Checks.

. . . couldn't write his name?

Tyrannosaurus X.

Why did the referee kick Ankylosaurus out of the football game?

He kept spiking the ball.

What did the impudent young Allosaurus call his grandfather?

An old fossil.

Where did Deinonychus get her nails done?

At the talon salon.

What abruptly woke the young Herrerasaurus from her beauty sleep?

A dino-snore.

ARTIE: Have you heard any good dinosaur jokes?
LEAH: Dinosaur jokes are old!
ARTIE: Old!? They're extinct!

Why was the Abelisaurus excited to see the dentist?

She had a *filling* that dentists were delicious.

The fossil remains of which two fierce dinosaurs were found side by side in ancient Persia?

Tehran-osaurus Rex and Iran-osaurus Rex.

Knock, knock.

Who's there?

Who.

Who who?

Who . . . who . . . who left the door unlocked with a vicious Velociraptor knocking?!

What's a dinosaur's favorite piece of Christmas music?

"The Hallelujah 'Saurus."

Why did the Ultrasaurus need a bandage?

She had a dino-sore.

What did the duck-billed Hadrosaurus say when purchasing some lipstick?

"Put it on my bill."

What do you call a sluggish fossil?

Lazybones.

What happened when the Tyrannosaurus gobbled up the mediocre comic?

He felt a little funny.

HA HA HA HA HA HA

What do you call a Pachycephalosaurus who is very particular about what she eats?

A Picky-cephalosaurus.

ARTIE: Which fossils are readily found in Mongolia?
LEAH: Mongolian ones.

What did the sauropod say to the theropod?

"Hey, do you want to grab a bite?"

What was the true identity of the mild-mannered Kentrosaurus whose alter ego was Supersaurus?

Clark Kentrosaurus.

What do you call a Dryosaurus who got caught in the rain?

A wet Dryosaurus.

What's it called when Tyrannosaurus comes upon his supper in an entertaining way?

A meat cute.

What do guests wipe their feet on before entering Diplodocus's lair?

A Diplo-mat.

What footwear did basketball-playing horned dinosaurs favor?

Tricera-high-tops.

What was Apatosaurus's favorite old-time TV quiz show?

Stomp the Stars.

What do you say to a charging Odontosaurus?

"Oh, don't!"

Why were Brachiosauruses so slow to apologize?

It took them a long time to swallow their pride.

What did the baby T. Rex ask for after being fed an Ornitholestes by his mom?

"*More*-nitholestes, please!"

Why would you never want to borrow money from a T. Rex?

They engage in predatory lending.

LEAH: Was Apatosaurus fat?
ARTIE: Naaah, just big-boned.

What did the creationist say when he was asked if he knew any good dinosaur jokes?

"They don't exist."

If a male Tyrannosaurus Rex is known as the "King of the Dinosaurs," what's a female Tyrannosaurus Rex?

King of the Dinosaurs.

What should you do if a Dromaeosaurus starts to devour a dictionary?

Take the words right out of his mouth.

Why would you never want Argentinosaurus, the heaviest dinosaur, to be smitten with you?

She'll have a crush on you.

How did the absolute smartest dinosaurs graduate college?

With extinction!

What do you call a Dromaeosaurus whose name is spelled the same forward and backward?

A Palin-dromaeosaurus.

HA HA HA HA HA

How do you make a Gallimimus float?

Put two scoops of ice cream in a glass of root beer. Then add one Gallimimus and stir vigorously.

Did you hear about the lethargic Leptoceratops who just dragged himself along?

He was more of a *Shlep*-toceratops.

What *always* followed the Diplodocus?

His tail.

What did the tanklike Edmontosaurus say upon getting a compliment?

"Tanks a lot!"

Why should you never slow-dance when Triceratops are around?

Because they keep horning in.

ARTIE: Why was Albertosaurus eating constantly?
LEAH: I'm not really sure. But she *was* a *dine*-osaur.

Who did the young Therizinosaurus wait up all night for on Christmas Eve?

Santa Claws.

Which dinosaur had a lung condition?

Bronchiosaurus.

Where did the Nodosaurus purchase all of her sundries?

At the dino-store.

Why was the hungry Spinosaurus happy when it came upon a tasty hadrosaur taking a nap?

It was a sight for *'saur* eyes!

What did the Brachiosauruses do on their date?

They necked.

What makes Tyranno-sore?

Too much *Rex*-ercise.

Did the film *Jurassic Park* do well at the box office?

Yes, it was a roaring success!

How did the Tyrannosaurus fare at boxing?

She became the heavyweight *chomp*!

What would an Ankylosaurus say before swinging his fearsome tail at a predator?

"Welcome to the club!"

Which dinosaur was entirely sightless?

Never-saur-us.

How do we know the Stegosaurus was overscheduled?

He had a lot on his plates.

LEAH: Did you know that Baryonyx had a hooked thumb claw to distinguish it from the other dinosaurs?
ARTIE: No, but I imagine it stuck out like a 'saur thumb.

What did carbon dating reveal about the Apatosaurus?

That he had a big carbon footprint.

Which dinosaurs were born to build?

Lego-sauruses.

Gobbling up so many cars adversely affected which structures in Troodon's DNA?

His chrome-osomes.

Which dinosaurs were into hip-hop?

Rap-tors.

What were grown specifically for Protoceratops to eat?

Protocera-crops.

What do you call a dinosaur that ate only boundary bushes?

A *hedge*-atarian.

And one that ate only the borders of her food and threw away the rest?

An *edge*-atarian.

What was the ugliest prehistoric creature?

The Eye-saur.

How would you describe a tuckered-out Gastonia?

Out of gas.

Which early reptiles ate extra salt to avoid deficiencies?

Iodine-osaurs.

Which horned dinosaur had a knack for publicity?

Promo-ceratops.

Were Barosauruses known to be risk-takers?

Yes, they would stick their necks out.

Why didn't dinosaurs fly?

It was way over their heads.

What do you call an Allosaurus who's a great big coward?

A Marshmallo-saurus!

Which dinosaur was partial to pancakes?

Tri-*syrup*-tops.

What was the favorite playground equipment of young prehistoric reptiles?

The dino-see-saur.

Where did Coelophysis and her friends go to sunbathe?

The dino-shore.

If a coprolite is a piece of fossilized dino poop, what would you call a weighty pile of Titanosaurus dung?

Copro-*heavy*!

Was the Ultrasaurus a healthy dinosaur?

Yes, ultra-sound.

What did the Gorgosaurus say after he was fed a tasty snack?

"Thanks a munch!"

Was Triceratops known to be a boastful dinosaur?

Yes, he would toot his own horn.

Where did Diplodocus buy most of his apparel?

Big-and-tall shops.

Knock, knock.

Who's there?

You.

You who?

Yoo-hoo, there are no dinosaurs around anymore to chase us!

How was a Dryosaurus fossil classified?

Bone Dry.

Why didn't the Tyrannosaurus skeleton lunge at the museum visitors?

Because she had no guts!

LEAH: Any idea how long dinosaurs lived?

ARTIE: Hmm. I would think about the same as *short* dinosaurs.

Did you hear about the two long-necked dinosaurs that were utterly indistinguishable?

They were like two peas in a sauropod.

Which gentle giant had a literary flair?

The Brontë-saurus.

What did the Spinosaurus that was unlucky in love sign up for?

Carbon dating.

What happens to a dinosaur fossil after a heavy thunderstorm?

It gets soaked to the bone.

What did the other dinos call the Protoceratops that was new to the neighborhood?

A greenhorn.

What do you call a Troodon that gobbles up trousers?

A *pant*-eater.

What's a Polacanthus that just reeled in his dinner?

A fishing Pole-acanthus.

What are dinosaur bathrooms decorated with?

Rep-*tiles*.

What do you call the remains of prehistoric creatures that acted like dunderheads?

Fossil fools!

What do you call a Gastonia that has just read this joke book?

A laughing Gas-tonia.

Why did Deinonychus, with his razor-like teeth and claws, put on his finest suit?

Because he was a sharp dresser.

When their babies had the flu, who would theropods take them to see?

The biped-iatrician.

What do you call a tedious Torosaurus?

A dino-*bore*.

Which long-necked dinosaur with a walnut-size brain favored physical strength over intelligence?

The *Brawn*-tosaurus.

In which national park were fossils of many misbehaving dinosaurs found?

The Badlands.

ARTIE: Was it true that Triceratops was the most successful of the dinosaurs?

LEAH: Yes, they were Tricera-*tops* in their field!

What was an Ankylosaurus's favorite suit of cards?

Clubs!

Which dinosaur had a penchant for golf?

Tee Rex.

What do you say when you meet a two-headed Tarbosaurus?

"Hello, hello."

Why did the Diplodocus gobble up the factory?

Well, she *was* a *plant*-eater.

What did the Supersaurus waiter ask the diners?

"Soup or 'saurus?"

LEAH: Are uncleaned fossils less expensive to buy?

ARTIE: Yeah, I hear they're dirt cheap.

Which dinosaur engaged in espionage?

Spy-nosaurus.

Why was the Microraptor tossed out of the Micro-film?

Her Micro-phone kept going off.

What do you call a vain Allosaurus?

A Shallo-saurus.

Why did the dinosaur eat a transistor radio?

She was fond of sound bites.

What did they call the most mischievous student at Jurassic Park Elementary?

The class clone.

Was it easy to collect a large pile of coprolites?

No, it was heavy-doody.

What do scientists call a prehistoric reptile who lacked pigment?

An albino-saur.

Who watched the young Psittacosaurus when his parents were out scaring up some dinner?

The baby-Psitta!

Why do the fossilized heads of the Camptosaurus not feel any pain?

They're *numb* skulls.

HA HA HA HA HA HA HA HA

Which dinosaur used an ointment from a native plant to treat her sunburn?

Aloe-saurus.

How did the Diplodocus race end?

They finished neck and neck.

LEAH: Even trees were said to tremble with terror when Tyrannosaurus Rex stalked by.
ARTIE: Yeah, I believe that's where we get petrified wood.

Where would the Ankylosaurus go for a little rest and relaxation?

Club Med.

Which dinosaur roared in the highest vocal range?

Soprano-saurus Rex!

What did the Maiasaura say when she walked into a café?

"Ouch!"

What do you have when two Parasaurolophuses get married?

A pair o' saurolophuses.

Why did the prehistoric creature have to sit by the fire?

He was a cold 'saur.

How did Gorgosaurus feel about Patagosaurus?

It was love at first bite.

Which dinosaurs had the best time on Father's Day?

Tricera-pops.

Was the sail-backed Dimetrodon effective on the baseball mound?

Yes, he had a good sail's pitch.

Why did the rapacious Troodon enter a church?

She was in search of pray.

Which luxury car did Tyrannosaurus prefer to drive?

A Rexus.

What would you call an Apatosaurus at bat?

A heavy hitter.

Why would other dinosaurs fall asleep when Diplodocus told a story?

She had a very long tale.

Where could Protoceratops purchase accessories for her horns?

At Protocera-shops.

What was as big as a Titanosaurus but weighed nothing?

His shadow!

Why was dino dung so variable?

Different species, different feces.

What do scientists call a Polacanthus who is far too thin?

A Beanpole-acanthus.

Where are dinosaur bones that have been exposed to radiation held?

At a nuclear fossility.

What was the most impressive dinosaur?

Tyrannosaurus Rocks!

Which fearsome predator had antlers?

Tyrannosaurus Racks!

Did the Gastonia enjoy life?

Yes, he thought it was a gas.

Why did the dinosaurs from *Jurassic Park* constantly prank each other?

They were always cloning around.

Where on Long Island could many Brachiosauruses be found?

Great Neck.

ARTIE: Did you hear about the armored dinosaur that got caught out in a big rainstorm?

LEAH: Poor thing. He's now an Ankylosau-*rust*.

What does a Triceratops sit on?

Her Tricera-*bottom*!

Did Tyrannosaurus make a good accountant?

Yes, she could sure crunch numbers.

What was the Ultrasaurus's favorite flower?

An Ultra-violet.

Why did the Hesperornis cross the road?

Because the chicken hadn't evolved yet.

Did the Brachiosaurus's debut album do well?

It was a smash!

What did Pelecanimimus have that no other dinosaur had?

Baby Pelecanimimus!

How do you encourage an Oviraptor?

You egg her on.

What was Tyrannosaurus's favorite ice-skating maneuver?

A figure ate!

How do we know that dinosaurs enjoyed good dental hygiene?

From their flossils.

What type of sweaters did T. Rex favor?

V-nex.

What do you call a thieving duck-billed Hadrosaurus?

A robber ducky.

Who led the Microraptor baseball team?

The Micro-manager.

HA HA HA HA HA

How were Velociraptors described when they fell in love?

They were said to be en-raptored.

LEAH: What family does Gargoyleosaurus belong to?
ARTIE: I don't think *any* families in the neighborhood have one.

What did the teenage Troodon fear when he forgot to charge his cell phone?

That his social life would be extinct.

What was the dinosaurs' favorite dance craze?

The Stomp.

How do we know Stegosauruses had a hearty appetite?

They always cleaned their plates.

Who was in love with Djulietosaurus?

Dromaeosaurus.

What language did the "tyrant king" Tyrannosaurus Rex speak?

The King's English.

Where do you find Compsognathus?

Well, it depends on where you lost it.

Why did the Triceratops want to take revenge on the Protoceratops?

He had a dino-score to settle.

What do you call a dull and boring Dryptosaurus?

A Dryp.

What was the constellation that resembled a Supersaurus composed of?

Superstars!

What's an Apatosaurus's favorite vegetable?

Squash.

Why did the duck-billed Hadrosaurus get in trouble?

He had a fowl mouth.

Was Edmontosaurus under some strain when a T. Rex was near?

Yes, she could feel the crunch.

ARTIE: Did you hear about the Lambeosaurus who broke out of jail?

LEAH: I sure did! He's on the lam.

What was the Parasaurolophus's favorite brand of toothpaste?

Crest.

What did certain dinosaurs use as paper currency?

Duckbills!

Why did the Allosaurus hunt in family groups?

Because the family that preys together stays together.

Why would Pachycephalosaurus head-butt his foes?

He was a butthead.

What would an Ankylosaurus typically have for lunch?

A club sandwich.

Did you hear about the Styracosaurus who looked for his lost neck fringe?

He became a frill seeker.

Were dinosaurs the life of the party?

Yes, they were TONS of fun!

What has eight legs, six horns, and four eyes?

A Triceratops looking in the mirror!

What do you call a museum exhibit that shows dinosaurs being killed by predators?

Die-oramas.

LEAH: Did you hear about the Tyrannosaurus who boarded a plane?

ARTIE: She had a first-class meal.

MAMMAL MERRIMENT

Why did Megatherium, the giant prehistoric ground sloth, have an inseparable friend?

They were cut from the same sloth.

What's it called when Megatherium nudges you along?

A slow poke.

Knock, knock.
> Who's there?

Saber-toothed tiger.
> Saber-toothed tiger who?

Saber-toothed tiger Jones.
> Well, why didn't ya say so? Come on in.

What do you call a Glyptodon (an early armadillo) with a viselike handshake?
> A Grip-todon.

Did Eohippus, the dawn horse, move from place to place?
> No, she preferred a stable environment.

Where did Josephoartigasia, the ancient rodent, live?
> In a mouse pad.

What was the name of the fellow who was attacked by a saber-toothed tiger?
> Claude!

What was the favorite fruit of the ancient ape Gigantopithecus?
> Ape-ricots!

Knock, knock.
Who's there?
Aaaaah.
Aaaaah who?
Aaaaah-woooooo!!!!!
It's the dire wolf. Run for your lives!

Why did the prehistoric cave bear with humongous teeth complain so much whenever he had a toothache?
He just couldn't *bear* the pain.

There were two Smilodons lurking in the forest. One of them says, "Grrrrrr!" The other says, "Hey, that's what I was going to say."

Which fierce member of the cat family had a face that often expressed joy?
The Smile-odon.

What did the mama Eohippus say to her foal?
"It's pasture bedtime."

How does a cave bear show affection?
With a bear hug.

Which saber-toothed explorer searched for the Fountain of Youth?

Pounce de León.

LEAH: What do you call a saber-toothed tiger with three eyes?

ARTIE: Hmm. A saber-toothed *tiiiger*!

Did the dire wolf ever get angry?

Yes, howling mad.

What do you say to a sad Eohippus?

"Why the long face?"

How were particularly savage early mammals described?

Fur-ocious.

What do you call a nearsighted Uintatherium that forgot to wear his glasses?

A Squint-atherium.

How would the dire wolf react to a sentimental movie?

He would cry wolf.

Which extinct big cat really enjoyed his meals?

The savor-toothed tiger.

Why was the giant extinct primate Gigantopithecus beloved by all?

She was a great ape.

What was a Megatherium clergyman also known as?

A man of the sloth.

ARTIE: Did you hear the story about the runaway Eohippus?
LEAH: I didn't. But I imagine it was a tale of *whoa*!

What do you call a cave bear that failed to take care of his teeth?

A gummy bear.

How many dire wolves can fit in an empty den?

One. After that, it isn't empty anymore.

What do you call a Megatherium chef?

A slow cooker.

How did the dire wolf prepare for an overnight trip?

He would wolf pack.

Would cave bears endure unpleasantness with grace?

Yes, they would grin and bear it.

What was the favorite footwear of Eohippus?

Saddle shoes.

How can you tell when a saber-toothed tiger is in a good mood?

She has a little pounce in her step.

Whose trade involved the coloring of cloth in prehistoric times?

The dyer wolf.

Why did the saber-toothed tiger follow his mate over the cliff?

He was a copycat!

What did the dire wolf wear to the costume party?

Sheep's clothing.

How was the buffalo-size Josephoartigasia, the largest prehistoric rodent, described?

Enormouse!

ARTIE: Why didn't cave bears wear shoes?
LEAH: What difference would it make? They'd still have bear feet.

What's an Eohippus pony with a sore throat?

A little hoarse.

What do you call a cave bear during the Ice Age?

A cave *brrr*.

Who was the ancient rodent Josephoartigasia's favorite Russian composer?

Mouse-sorgsky.

Where would the dire wolf go to borrow money?

The loan wolf.

What would happen when Gigantopithecus, a giant extinct ape, got mad?

He'd go ape.

What do you call a comfy cave and some square meals?

The bear necessities.

What ferocious member of the cat family lived right next door?

The neighbor-toothed tiger.

MAD SCIENCE

Which branch of science takes its name from the simple bucket that's used for digging up dinosaur fossils?

Pail-eontology.

What do fossil finders spread on their sandwiches?

Preserves.

What did the beatnik fossil hunter ask his helpers?

"Can you dig it, man?"

In what rocks do we find fossils from lazy dinosaurs?

Sedentary rocks!

What is it called when two famed fossil hunters argue over the source of a fossil?

A bone of contention.

Where do paleontologists search for dormant dinosaur bones?

In fossil beds.

What did scientists who dismissed the notion that dinosaurs could blend in with their surroundings call it?

Sham-ouflage.

What do paleontologists go out on in search of Tyrannosauruses?

Rex-peditions!

HA HA HA HA HA

Silly Science

Which type of scientists excavated the site of the world's earliest dog?

Bark-eologists.

And which discovered and excavated Noah's ship?

Ark-eologists.

Which subgroup of scientists felt the popular theories about why dinosaurs disappeared were sheer nonsense?

Malarkey-ologists.

We know geologists study rocks and scatologists study fossilized dino poop. What do we call scientists who study "number one"?

Pee-ologists.

Which branch of science discovered Megalodon, the extinct giant shark?

Shark-eology.

What's a great first name for a paleontologist?

Doug.

Which scientists could be snide with their colleagues?

Snarky-ologists.

Scientists find this upper arm bone even funnier than the funny bone.

The humerus!

What branch of earth science is filled with surprises?

Gee-ology.

What happens to scientists who spend too much time studying prehistoric wetlands?

They get bogged down.

Which scientists discovered that dinosaur societies were ruled by the females?

Matriarchy-ologists.

Did you hear about the exhausted paleontologist?

He worked his fingers to the bone.

Why was the archaeologist doubled over with laughter?

He was digging when he hit the funny bone.

How do scientists refer to the landmass where the dinosaurs lived during bouts of global warming?

Frying Pan-gaea.

What would paleontology students request after studying too much morphology?

Less-phology!

Museum Mirth

Where can you find fossils of the very first cows?

In the *Moo*-seum of Natural History.

Where can you find fossils of the earliest snakes?

The Museum of Natural *Hissss*-tory.

Where in Washington, D.C., can you learn about the legends surrounding dinosaurs?

The Myth-sonian.

In which cultural institution can you find the ghosts of early hunter-gatherers?

The Museum of Supernatural History!

Do paleontologists enjoy what they do?

Yes, they dig their work.

Did you hear about the dinosaur hunter who argued with his colleague?

Yes, he had a bone to pick with him.

Are the conditions of some dinosaur bones disappointing to their discoverers?

Yes, sometimes they're not all they're cracked up to be.

What is the favorite seasoning of earth scientists?

Geologic thyme.

Speculation that the bony plates on the back of Stegosaurus would sometimes shift when they craned their necks gave rise to which scientific theory?

Plate *neck*-tonics!

How did scientists describe the world's stupidest fossil?

Boneheaded.

HA

EARLY HUMAN HUMOR

How was Mrs. Australopithecus, the earliest human, referred to?

The First Lady.

What do you say when you see an adorable baby Australopithecus?

"*Awwwwww-stralopithecus!*"

Where did the caveman keep his pool table and jumbo TV?

In his man cave.

What was a popular pickup line among Neanderthal men?

"You're the hottest thing since fire."

What rather specialized category of prehistoric creatures fed solely on cavemen named Herbie?

Herbie-vores!

What do you call a caveman with bad posture?

A concave man!

When do cave boys and girls get to practice their vowels?

When they're being pursued by a voracious Velociraptor! (*Aaaiiiiieeeee!*)

What did the caveman say when he slid down the Brachiosaurus's neck and departed?

"Sooooo long!"

Which early humans lived a nomadic lifestyle?

Meander-thals.

What do you call the prehistoric periodicals, such as *Lava Today,* that featured the latest volcano news?

Magma-zines.

Who was one of the most popular Neanderthal presidents?

Hairy S. Truman.

Knock, knock.

Who's there?

Cave boy.

Cave boy who?

Cave . . . boy, it's cold out here. Lemme in!

Did cavemen wax nostalgic about the first time they made fire?

Yes, they never forgot their old flames.

What did the sign on the wall of the Neanderthal family's dwelling say?

Cave, sweet cave.

How were very proper early women described?

Prim-itive.

What do cavemen and hipsters have in common?

They both like to go clubbing.

Who was the Neanderthal teen's favorite fantasy figure?

Hairy Potter!

HA HA HA HA HA

Was the caveman trustworthy?

He was a caveman of his word.

Why did the naughty Australopithecus have his mouth washed out with Lava soap?

To stop him from Australopithe-cussing!

LEAH: Was Cro-Magnon man resistant to change?
ARTIE: Yes, he much preferred the status *Cro.*

How were the ghosts of early humans categorized?

Haunter-gatherers.

What did the dinosaur-steak-loving caveman wear as a bib?

A sir-loin cloth.

ARTIE: Did you hear about the caveman who trapped a ferocious dinosaur?
LEAH: Yeah, he was a raptor captor.

Was Cro-Magnon man a cannibal?

No, they never ate Cro.

HA HA HA HA HA

What subject could cave people never major in?

History.

Which was the paper of record among Australopithecus?

The Prehistoric Times.

Which early humans had a healthy glow?

Neon-derthals.

What did cavemen use to carve up their massive meals?

A dino-*saw.*

LEAH: Did the first Cro-Magnon pilot choose a direct flight pattern?

ARTIE: Yes, he went straight as the Cro flies.

Television sets of cavemen were *always* tuned to this popular station.

The Prehistory Channel.

Did some early humans pray?

Yes, they could be seen on bended *knee*-anderthals.

ARTIE: Would early humans *always* stand up for their rights?

LEAH: Well, sometimes they'd cave in.

What do you call an Australopithecus who can't find his way home?

A *Lost*-stralopithecus.

Why would early humans relieve themselves in active volcanoes?

That was their *lava*-tory.

Which upright early human lived in the shadow of an active volcano?

Homo eruptus.

LEAH: Why did the Cro-Magnon man *crown* the Tyrannosaurus Rex with his club?

ARTIE: Because he was King of the Dinosaurs.

49

Why did the Neanderthal man feel that the Neanderthal woman's place was in the cave?

He wasn't very evolved.

What do you call an Australopithecus who is bone-tired?

An Exhaust-stralopithecus.

Would nomadic early humans miss the bristlecones after leaving the woods?

Yes, they would often pine for them.

What did the vain Neanderthal man work on?

His Neander-tan.

Did the sick caveman improve after eating healing plants?

Yes, he took a *fern* for the better.

Would cavemen avoid coming into contact with Tyrannosauruses?

Yes, they wouldn't touch them with a ten-foot Polacanthus.

Why did the Australopithecus prefer to build her hut near a volcano?

She was in lava with the scenery.

What song did the Neanderthal woman sing to her Neanderthal man?

"I'm Just Wild About Hairy."

What was the favorite dessert of Australopithecus?

Australopithe-custard!

Which early human actually designed the first airplane with an escape mechanism?

Homo ejectus.

ARTIE: Do you know anything about the background of the caveman who invented fire?
LEAH: No, but he must have had a really dark past.

How did the Neanderthal man lose his pendulous paunch?

The Paleo Diet.

What do you call an Australopithecus with an active social life?

A caveman-about-town.

Did you hear about the brilliant Cro-Magnon woman who was at the top of her class?

She graduated *magnon* cum laude!

AN OCEAN OF LAUGHTER

Would Megalodon, the giant ancient shark, take a wee nip out of you if you were swimming nearby?

No, he would take a *Mega*-bite!

Was the ancient crocodilian Sarcosuchus able to make a phone call?

No, she couldn't get a croco-dial tone.

Why were trilobites considered shy?

They wouldn't come out of their shells.

What was the most disgusting large marine reptile?

The *Ick*-thyosaurus.

Which Sarcosuchus family was fabulously wealthy?

The Croc-efellers.

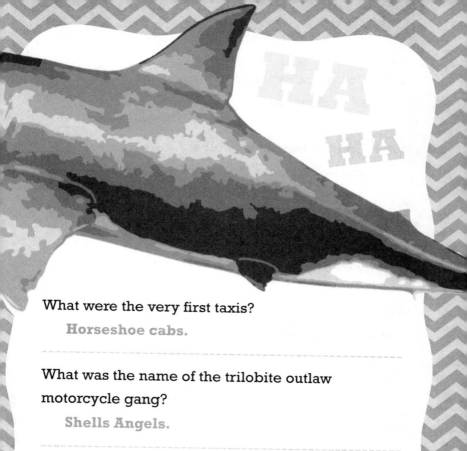

What were the very first taxis?

Horseshoe cabs.

What was the name of the trilobite outlaw motorcycle gang?

Shells Angels.

Why were pliosaurs found in salt water?

Because pepper made them sneeze.

What do you call a Mosasaurus who moves in a leisurely manner?

A *Mosey*-saurus.

What do trilobites do on their birthdays?

They shell-ebrate!

What do you call a female Elasmosaurus?

A *She*-lasmosaurus.

Why did the Plesiosaurus blush?

Because she saw the ocean's bottom.

ARTIE: Did you hear about the giant fish that swam ashore to destroy Tokyo?
LEAH: Do you mean *Cod*-zilla?

Why would you never want to drive your car behind a long-necked Elasmosaurus?

Too many rubber-necking delays!

Is it true that Sarcosuchus was one of the largest of the extinct birds?

No, that's a croc!

What daily supplement keeps a coelacanth feeling his best?

Vitamin Sea.

HA HA HA HA HA
HA HA HA HA HA

Who was the favorite children's book author of the early nautiloids?

Shell Silverstein.

Why did the early humans suspect that the coelacanth had stolen their food?

Because something fishy was going on.

How did the fisherman feel when he hauled in a Megalodon?

He got the shark of his life.

How does a coelacanth wait for a tasty meal?

With baited breath.

Which was the most polite of the ancient marine reptiles?

The *Please*-iosaurus.

What did Megalodon experience when he swam off to an unfamiliar sea?

Culture shark.

How would you characterize trilobites when a hungry predator swam by?

Shell-shocked.

LEAH: Did you hear about the Sarcosuchus with a sweet tooth for candy bars?

ARTIE: No, but I bet she was a real choco-dile!

Did the first fisherman to haul in a coelacanth, which was thought to be extinct, doubt the identity of his incredible catch?

Yes, but he concluded it was the *reel* thing.

What was the preferred snack of Elasmosaurus?

Trilo-bites.

What did Megalodon experience when he went to price a new car?

Sticker shark!

A ZANY MISCELLANY

What do you use on Meganeura, the largest flying insect ever?

The largest fly swatter ever!

Which tiny creatures bedeviled the ancient reptiles?

Dino-mites.

Where were the preserved remains of many prehistoric peaches and cherries found?

The La Brea Tar Pits.

It took backbone for this category of prehistoric animals to change their religion.

Convert-ebrates.

What do we call gargantuan igneous rocks?

BIG-neous rocks.

What are foolish cave explorers called?

Spe-lunkheads.

LEAH: What would you compare mosses and other early lifeforms to?

ARTIE: I would liken them to lichen.

Which ancient insects grew so big they could tote their food?

Draggin' flies.

What were those massive prehistoric pigs called?

Swine-osaurs.

Where were the earliest lifeforms imprisoned if they committed criminal acts?

In a single cell.

How would ancient insects travel when they wanted to conserve their energy?

By buggy.

Cycads, the most cunning of the earliest plants, were also known as what?

Sly-cads.

Which animals had the backbone to try to attract a mate?

Flirt-ebrates.

Which early amphibians lived in caves?

Frog-lodytes.

What prehistoric insect that's still with us today could tell time?

Clock-roach.

A collision with this disagreeable meteor may have been responsible for the extinction of the dinosaurs.

A *nasty*-roid.

Why did invertebrates always get along?

Because they didn't have a mean bone in their bodies.

Why did the laboratory bacteria cross the Petri dish?

To get to the other slide.

What were the prehistoric forerunners of some very common picnic pests called?

Ant-cestors.

ARTIE: Which class of animals was known to fudge the truth?

LEAH: You must be referring to the am-*fib*-ians.

A PACK OF PACHYDERM PUNS

Leah: **What do you call a woolly mammoth who just got a haircut?**

ARTIE: A not-so-woolly mammoth.

What was an ancient pachyderm's favorite church service?

Midnight Mass-todon.

Knock, knock.

Who's there?

Mammoth.

Mammoth who?

Mammoth love babyeth!

Did you hear about the Platybelodon, an early elephant, who felt that her elongated proboscis was a tad *too* long?

She had it trunk-cated.

What do you call a harsh mastodon boss?

A real tusk-master.

Were mammoths easily fooled?

Yes, you could pull the wool over their eyes.

What do you get when you cross a coelacanth and a mastodon?

Swimming trunks!

Why would you never give a challenging assignment to the early elephant Gomphotherium?

He wouldn't be up to the tusk.

Who taught the precocious pachyderms during prehistoric times?

The schoolmaster-don.

What did the police do after woolly mammoths rampaged through town?

They combed the area for suspects.

Where in Italy would mastodons go for vacation?

Tusk-any.

Which pesky insect fed on the fur of prehistoric pachyderms?

The woolly mam-*moth.*

Who was in charge of the mail during prehistoric times?

The postmaster-don.

Which prehistoric pachyderms picked on the other species?

Bully mammoths.

Why did the Platybelodons have wrinkled skin?

Because they didn't fit on an ironing board.

ARTIE: How does a mammoth express annoyance?
LEAH: She says, "Tusk, tusk!"

Why were the young mastodons red-faced with embarrassment?

They had gone swimming and lost their trunks.

Which was the cleverest of the early elephants?

The wily mammoth.

And which loved to pull stunts on his motorcycle?

The wheelie mammoth.

What was the early elephant Gomphotherium's favorite genre of literature?

Ele-phantasy!

Who left a quarter under the pillow of the young mastodon?

The Tusk Fairy.

Platybelodons in retail frequently attended what kind of events to meet their suppliers?

Trunk shows.

LEAH: Were mastodons hard workers?
ARTIE: Yes, they worked from dawn to tusk.

What do you give an overexcited Gomphotherium?

Trunk-quilizers.

Who supervised the den leaders in prehistoric times?

The scoutmaster-don.

What would woolly mammoths pack before they migrated?

Their trunks.

Which early elephant was known to hoard food?

Amass-todon.

What makes this unusual noise: "*CHHH-CHHH-CHHH*-PTOOEY!!!*"*?

A saber-toothed tiger with a mammoth furball.

THE FORECAST IS FOR FUNNY SKIES

What does a Pteranodon get after flying too long?

Ptired.

Which was the scariest flying reptile?

The Terror-dactyl!

Was Archaeopteryx proud when she graduated with honors?

Yes, she saw it as a feather in her cap.

Do Pteranodons study hard for a test?

No, they just wing it.

How do you upset an Archaeopteryx?

You ruffle her feathers.

Why can't you hear a Pterodactyl when he's using the toilet?

Because the *p* is silent.

Which pterosaur had wings yet could not fly?

A dead one!

Did you hear about the Pteranodon who was successful at work?

Yes, he earned his wings.

How did the Marshosaurus feel after eating his first Archaeopteryx?

Down in the mouth!

What was the Pterodactyl's favorite gangster movie?

Bonnie and Glide.

When were hungry pterosaurs like turkeys?

When they gobbled.

After crashing into the caveman's home, what did the Rhamphorhynchus become?

A battering Rham.

Why did the Archaeopteryx catch the worm?

Because she was an early bird.

ARTIE: Who helps a Pterodactyl find a girlfriend?
LEAH: His wingman.

How did the headline in the *Prehistoric Post* read when a Rhamphorhynchus was spotted flying over L.A.?

DINO SOARS!

Why was the Pterodactyl so nervous when she performed onstage?

Another was waiting in the wings.

Why was the Archaeopteryx all abuzz with social activity?

She liked to make the Pleisto-*scene*!

What do you call it when Pterodactyls have a noisy party?

A wing-ding.

A STITCH . . . IN TIME

Who played the bugle during military funerals in prehistoric times?

Tricera-*taps*.

When were dinosaurs at their most friendly?

During a Nice Age.

Why were dinosaurs frequently tardy?

Because they lived in the *Late* Cretaceous period.

Which dinosaur waitress made money earning gratuities in prehistoric times?

Tricera-*tips*.

Which early period of time saw great progress leading up to the next period?

The Stepping-Stone Age.

How did mothers discipline unruly tots during the Carboniferous period?

They would rake them over the coals.

What was the favorite hotdog garnish during prehistoric times?

'Saur-kraut.

During what period were many small, rich pastries consumed?

The Scone Age.

When were cavemen at the greatest risk of getting a sunburn?

During the Pale-eozoic era.

What created a Dust Bowl in prehistoric times?

Loose Tricera-topsoil.

What nursery rhyme was very popular during the Carboniferous period?

"Old King Coal."

What was the most popular boys' name back in the Proterozoic eon?

Proterozoic Leon!

When were dinosaurs at their most slovenly?

During the *Mess*-ozoic era.

LEAH: Were sons like their daddies during the Carboniferous period?

ARTIE: Yes, carbon copies!

Who was the head of the crime syndicate in prehistoric times?

The Iguano-*Don.*

During which geological period were dinosaurs overly concerned about having curly hair?

The *Perm*-ian.

HA HA HA HA HA
HA HA HA HA HA

Who upheld the law during prehistoric times?

Tricera-cops.

What's a time line?

A wrinkle in time.

How were youngsters classified during the Carboniferous period?

Coal minors.

Which automobile revolutionized transportation during prehistoric times?

The Model T. Rex.

Where did people sleep during the Carboniferous period?

Coal beds.

When did dinosaurs make their first attempt to fly?

During the *Try*-assic period.

Which period of time featured the very first rock band?

The Rolling Stone Age.

What was the most popular side dish during the Carboniferous period?

Coal slaw.

What was the name of the jalopy dealer in prehistoric times?

Tyrannosaurus Wrecks.

The Age of Dinosaurs was such an excellent time! What was the landmass they lived on known as?

A super continent.

What time is it when five ravenous Gorgosauruses pursue a single Centrosaurus?

Five after one.

Who wore an ascot in prehistoric times?

Tie-rannosaurus.

Which dinosaur had a wooden leg?

Peg-osaurus.

What was the most common zodiac sign among T. Rexes?

Tyranno-Taurus!

What do you call a prehistoric creature whose tootsies are tired?

Foot-saur.

RAWRR

Who was married to the Fada-burrasaurus?

The Muttaburrasaurus.

ARTIE: Why did the Ornithomimus gobble up the entire swim tournament?

LEAH: Well, after all, he *was* a meet-eater.

Which horned dinosaur's case had to go back before the court?

Retry-ceratops.

Though usually terribly aggressive, this dinosaur was sometimes an introvert.

The Shy-rannosaurus.

What do you call an extra-huge Argentinosaurus?

A *Large*-entinosaurus.

Why did T. Rex and Stegosaurus never talk about whose turn it was to take out the trash?

It was a 'saur point between them.

Who would prehistoric matadors confront in the ring?

Torosaurus.

Which dinosaur had a taste for the tango?

Dip-lodocus.

What do you call Tyrannosauruses who fail at everything?

Train Rex.

LEAH: Could the Supersaurus write her name?
ARTIE: Yes, in superscript.

Would Lagosuchus win a footrace?

No, often he would lag behind.

When flesh-eating dinosaurs got depressed, who treated them?

Theropod therapists.

What was the Ultrasaurus's favorite basketball team?

The Ultra-Sonics.

What do you call a Carnotaurus who gave up meat for whole grains?

A Carbo-taurus.

What did the surfing Microraptor hope for?

Micro-waves!

HA HA HA

What would you get when Diplodocuses were on the move?

A bottleneck!

How does the Protoceratops squeeze into her tight shoes?

She uses a shoehorn!

What do you call a Pachycephalosaurus with a screw loose?

A Wacky-cephalosaurus!

And how about one with *supremely* bad taste?

A Tacky-cephalosaurus.

How would you describe your situation if you were cornered by a hungry Allosaurus?

Crunch time.

ARTIE: Did you know that hadrosaurs lived in large packs for protection?
LEAH: Yes, I *herd*.

What was a musical Triceratops who was a whiz at playing his horns said to have?

Tricera-chops!

Who was Tyrannosaurus's favorite English actor?

Rex Harrison.

Did Stegosauruses volunteer their time for worthy causes?

Yes, they stepped up to the plate.

Why did the colossal titanosaurs make such good philosophers?

Because they were concerned about weighty matters.

Which dinosaur will always be remembered for fighting Davy Crockett?

The Alamosaurus.

What did the stressed-out Tyrannosaurus need?

A little Rex and relaxation.

What was Ankylosaurus's favorite baseball team?

The Yankee-losauruses!

And why would other teams not want to play against them?

It's said that they were 'saur losers.

How do you know when an Oviraptor is embarrassed?

She has egg on her face.

What do you get when you put all the bones of a dinosaur's head back together?

A skull-eton.

LEAH: How successful was the Tyrannosaurus who tried to become a vegetarian?

ARTIE: Well, he did the *beast* he could.

Did you hear about the witty duck-billed Anatotitan?

She was always making wise quacks.

Why do Ankylosauruses never need a golf caddie?

They take their clubs wherever they go.

What would Dilophosaurus wear for a job interview?

A double-crested jacket.

What did the ceratopsian do when she had to make a phone call?

She got on the horn.

How did Apatosaurus get to his job as a forester?

He just lumbered along.

Did pachycephalosaurs excel in school?

No, they were thick-headed dinosaurs.

How would you characterize a Tyrannosaurus Rex temper tantrum?

A fit for a king.

ARTIE: Would Styracosaurus sometimes get fed up with things?

LEAH: Yes, she would have her *frill* of it.

What do you call Patagosauruses who work on oil rigs?

Roughnecks.

What do you call a dinosaur who can bewitch with her spells?

A 'saur-ceress.

How do you know that the Oviraptor didn't do well at her recital?

They say she laid an egg.

HA

On which boat did Noah preserve two of every species of prehistoric creature?

The Jurassic Ark.

What was an Ankylosaurus's favorite cable channel?

Spike TV!

Was the sail-backed Dimetrodon a savvy shopper?

Yes, he always purchased items on sail.

LEAH: How many dinosaurs does it take to change a light bulb?
ARTIE: Only one. But he has to wait two hundred million years for the light bulb to be invented!

How would dinosaurs feel after moving their bowels?

Pooped.

Because the disappearance of the dinosaurs may have occurred somewhere around present-day Boston, scientists refer to the phenomenon as what?

Mass extinction.

What sound did the tedious Tyrannosaurus make?

A dull roar.

Can the Apatosaurus successfully negotiate a McDonald's drive-thru?

Yes, but it's a tall order.

How did dinosaur hunters refer to the bones of the largest titanosaur?

A colossal fossil.

Knock, knock.

Who's there?

Iguanodon.

Iguanodon who?

I gwana donut now!

What do you call a theropod on a bicycle?

A bi-pedaler.

Did the dino drill sergeant demand respect and obedience?

Yes, 'saur!

What was the horned dinosaur's favorite action film?

Tricera–Top Gun.

How do you know if you pass a Deinonychus?

You can't get the toilet seat down.

ARTIE: Here's a test. Can you name ten dinosaurs in ten seconds?

LEAH: Sure! Seven Stegosauruses and three Camptosauruses!

How does someone with a Cockney accent greet a vicious dinosaur?

"'Allo, 'saurus!"

What did dinosaurs serve on top of their spaghetti?

Tomato-saurus.

Why would football teams run up the score against the gentle Camptosaurus?

Because they were defenseless.

Why was Altirhinus, with its enlarged beak, so successful?

He was at the beak of his powers.

Which prehistoric creature got in trouble for using bad language?

The dino-swore.

How do you ask a dangerous dinosaur to an elegant lunch?

Tea, Rex?

What did the Argentinosaurus say when she brought her baby aboard the plane in her luggage?

"Boy, this suitcase weighs a ton!"

What did Diplodocus get for Father's Day?

Very long neckties.

When can *two* Alvarezsauruses use only *one* umbrella and not get wet?

When it's not raining.

Who was the dinosaurs' favorite Expressionist painter?

Edvard Munch.

What was it called when a Dryosaurus put an enchantment on you?

A Dry spell.

Why did Sinornithosaurus eat her food raw?

She never went to cooking school.

What was the best Supersaurus ever?

The Super-*duper*-saurus!

LEAH: What happened when the Barosaurus sat on a tricycle?

ARTIE: Nothing! The wheel hadn't been invented yet, let alone *three* wheels!

What's the most popular name given to Tyrannosaurus babies?

Rory.

Did the duck-billed Anatotitan hit a home run?

No, the ball went fowl.

What do you call an Edmontosaurus who is bleeding badly from a Majungasaurus bite?

A Redmontosaurus.

Which nursery rhyme did the juvenile Lambeosaurus love to recite?

"Mary Had a Little Lambeosaurus."

How did the Maiasaura skeleton know she was in love?

She felt it in her bones.

What kinds of sounds do Gorgosauruses make when they light the fireplace?

Bellows.

What would a polite Tyrannosaurus say when seated at the dinner table?

"Please pass the Saltasaurus."

Why do Ankylosauruses tend not to join outside organizations?

They have their own clubs.

What was an orange-haired horned dinosaur called?

Tricera-carrot-tops.

Which Late Cretaceous dinosaur was the star of a Disney cartoon?

Bambiraptor.

What do you call a larcenous Leptoceratops caught shoplifting?

A Klepto-ceratops!

How do you know if a Gorgosaurus is about to charge?

He asks if you accept MasterCard.

Why should you tiptoe around Gigantosaurus when he's napping?

You don't want to wake a sleeping giant.

Why would the Allosaurus catch a Tri-cereal-tops every morning?

Because it was the breakfast of *chomp*-ions!

Which dinosaur never had to ask for directions during migration?

Mapusaurus.

Why would theropods hungrily pursue the fleet-footed Gallimimus?

They liked fast food.

Why did Brachiosaurus have trouble finding jeans that fit?

He was too big for his britches.

Where would sauropods always feel right at home?

Long Island.

ARTIE: I'm lucky enough to have my own personal prehistoric pet.
LEAH: What do you call it?
ARTIE: Mine-osaur.

How did the dinosaur refer to his jammy pants?

His Tricera-bottoms.

Which sports car did the Lambeosaurus drive?

Lamborghini!

Why should you never go to a duck-billed Hadrosaurus if you're ill?

They're all quacks.

What do you do if you find a blue Corythosaurus?

Try to cheer her up.

Which dinosaur enjoyed riding the subway?

Di-*metro*-don.

We all know that meat-eating dinosaurs were referred to as carnivorous. But what do you call the few dinosaurs that subsisted solely on pinecones?

Cone-iferous.

Where would you find bullying behavior among dinosaurs?

Harass-ic Park.

HA HA HA

What do you call a prehistoric creature knighted by the queen?

Dino-sir.

LEAH: Which dinosaur made his home in ancient Ireland?

ARTIE: That would be a Pat O'Saurus.

How would you describe a horned dinosaur in a state of utter confusion?

Tricera-topsy-turvy!

What is a Megalosaurus who runs amok?

A Megalo-maniac!

Why did the Hypsilophodon curtail her consumption of cycads?

They went straight to her hyps.

Knock, knock.

Who's there?

Tyrannosauruses go.

Tyrannosauruses go who?

Nuh-uh. Owls go "hoo." Tyrannosauruses go "GRRRRRrrrrrrrrrrrr!"

What style kitchen did the Ultrasaurus prefer?

Ultra-modern.

Which horned dinosaur was always taking selfies?

Photo-ceratops.

What was Diplodocus's favorite nighttime camping treat?

Dino-s'mores!

What does a prehistoric reptile say when he apologizes?

"So 'saury."

How do you describe a dinosaur who was sprayed by a skunk but the smell has worn off?

Ex-stinked.

Why did the Tyrannosaurus gobble up his teacher?

Because he was hungry for knowledge.

What rank did the Argentinosaurus who joined the U.S. Army attain?

Sergeant-tinosaurus!

HA HA HA HA HA

What do you call an oddball Centrosaurus?

An Eccentro-saurus.

Which theme park cloned *only* long-necked dinosaurs?

Giraffic Park.

What do you get when you cross a horned dinosaur and a bunny?

Tricera-hops.

How do you get down from an Apatosaurus?

You don't. You get down from a goose.

Who was the favorite singer-songwriter of the Baryonyx?

Barry Manilow.

What would the duck-billed Hadrosaurus do when a hungry Quetzalcoatlus flew overhead?

Duck!

Why did the dinosaur's car come to a stop?

She got a flat tire-annosaurus.

HA HA HA HA HA

Why did Protoceratops travel in packs?

Because if they traveled in flocks, they surely would've been mistaken for sheep.

What do you give a Triceratops in acknowledgment of a job well done?

Her Tricera-props!

ARTIE: Could the Camarasaurus jump higher than a house?

LEAH: Sure. Houses can't jump.

What was Sauroposeidon's favorite apple drink?

Sauropo-cider.

What were prehistoric UFOs?

Dino-saucers.

How can you tell if there's an Argentinosaurus hiding out in your closet?

The door won't close.

HA HA HA HA HA
HA HA HA HA HA

How would you describe it when a Supersaurus is on the attack?

Super-charged.

Where did the sail-backed Spinosaurus pick up a replacement part?

At a garage sail.

What did prehistoric theater critics call disastrous performances by horned dinosaurs?

Tricera-flops.

What do you call a Stegosaurus who was financially successful?

Gold-plated.

What do you call a Camarasaurus using a wide-angle lens to take pictures?

A Camera-saurus.

What would you call a Gastonia after a meal of beans?

A Gassy-tonia.

Did the baby Dryptosaurus resemble his daddy?

Yes, he was a Dryp off the old block.

What do you say to a horned dinosaur after a valiant but failed effort?

"Nice try-ceratops."

What do you get when you cross an Allosaurus and a member of the crocodile family?

An Allo-gator.

Which superhero-engineered events often buried many dinosaurs?

Flash floods.

Which dinosaur was often teary-eyed?

Cry-olophosaurus.

Why were Tyrannosauruses considered truly wicked?

They were "prime evil."

How do you cheat a Triceratops?

You hornswoggle her.

How would you describe an ornithopod's proud accomplishment?

A beak achievement.

How do you raise a baby Gigantosaurus?

With a heavy-duty crane!

What was the favorite game of Majungasaurus?

Mah-jongg!

What do you get from a savage Carcharodontosaurus?

As far away as possible!

Which honest dinosaur wore a stovepipe hat?

Abe-lisaurus.

Why would the sickle-clawed Sinornithosaurus burst out laughing when you touched her?

Because she was very sicklish.

LEAH: Did you hear about the sail-backed Spinosaurus with the prize-winning appendage?
ARTIE: It was the sail of the century!

How would Spinosaurus react when she heard the roar of a fearsome Allosaurus?

It sent shivers down her spine.

Why would Torvosaurus let out a great big roar?

She hated small talk.

How does Microraptor rid himself of bad breath?

With Micro-Scope.

Was it true that Brachiosaurus was a deep thinker?

Yes, she was ponder-ous.

Which dinosaur rode a three-wheeled vehicle?

Tricycle-tops.

Why did the Barosaurus swing her tail?

Because there was no one else to swing it for her.

How do you keep a putrid Polacanthus from smelling?

Plug her nose!

How would you feel if you saw an Apatosaurus in your backyard?

Very, very old.

What do you call a Tyrannosaurus admiring himself in a mirror?

Double trouble!

Why would you *never* want a Herrerasaurus to owe you money?

She was a creditor predator.

What do you call a dinosaur that does nothing but lie out in the sun?

A *bask*-et case.

Why did Sauroposeidon, the tallest known dinosaur, get an advanced degree?

She believed in higher education.

Why was the Apatosaurus a whiz on Wall Street?

Because she was stock-y.

Which college football team did Triceratops always root for?

The Texas Longhorns.

What do you call the millennia-long reign of the Tyrannosauruses?

A dino dynasty.

Artie Bennett is an executive copy editor by day and a writer by night. In praise of his books for children, the *Huffington Post* wrote, "It appears there is no topic Mr. Bennett can't make funny and educational."

Artie is the author of a quartet of hilarious picture books: *The Butt Book*, winner of the Reuben Award; *Poopendous!*, his "number two" book; *Peter Panda Melts Down!*, an adorable departure from derrières and doo; and *Belches, Burps, and Farts—Oh My!* In addition, he has written two joke books, *The Universe's Greatest Dinosaur Jokes and Pre-Hysteric Puns* and *The Universe's Greatest School Jokes and Rip-Roaring Riddles*.

Artie and his wife, Leah, live in Brooklyn, New York, where Artie spends his time moving his car to satisfy the rigorous demands of alternate-side-of-the-street parking. Visit ArtieBennett.com . . . before someone else does!